Geography resources

KU-351-200

QFO
551

KU-351-200

01039

# LIFE IN THE
# PLAINS

Written by **Catherine Bradley**

Consultant Roger Hammond
*Director of Living Earth*

**FRANKLIN WATTS**
in association with
TWO-CAN

First published in this edition in 1991 by
Franklin Watts
96 Leonard Street
London EC2A 4RH

Copyright © Two-Can Publishing Ltd, 1991
Text copyright © Catherine Bradley, 1991
Design by Belinda Webster

Printed in Italy by Amadeus – Rome

All rights reserved. No part of this publication may be reproduced,
stored in a retrieval system or transmitted in any form or by any
means electronic, mechanical, photocopying, recording or otherwise,
without prior written permission of the copyright owner.

The JUMP! logo and the word JUMP!
are registered trade marks.

A CIP catalogue record for this book is available from the British Library

ISBN: 0-7496-0709-2

Photographic credits:
p.4-5 ZEFA/K. Bonath p.7 (top) Bruce Coleman/Andy Purcell (bottom) Bruce Coleman/Michael Freeman p.8 (top right and bottom left) Bruce Coleman/Gerald Cubitt p.9 Bruce Coleman/Peter Ward p.10 Bruce Coleman/Jane Burton p.11 Survival Anglia/J.B. Davidson p.12 (top right)Survival Anglia/Cindy Buxton (bottom left) Survival Anglia/Jen & Des Bartlett p.13 (top right) Ardea, London/Clem Haagner (bottom) ZEFA/Horus p.14 Bruce Coleman/Hans Reinhard p.15 (top right) Bruce Coleman/Norman Myers (bottom) Bruce Coleman/Gunter Ziesler p.16 Bruce Coleman/Dr Eckart Pott p.17 Planet Earth/Jonathan Scott p.18 Bruce Coleman/L.C. Marigo p.19 ZEFA/Leidmann p.20 Hutchison Library/Dr Nigel Smith p.21 (top right) Bruce Coleman/Mark N. Boulton (bottom) Bruce Coleman/D. Houston p.22 Survival Anglia/Richard & Julia Kemp p.23 Bruce Coleman/Simon Trevor

Front cover: Bruce Coleman/R.I.M. Campbell Back cover: NHPA/Peter Johnson

Illustrations by Michaela Stewart. Story by Claire Watts. Edited by Monica Byles.

# CONTENTS

All words marked in **bold** can be found in the glossary

# LOOKING AT THE PLAINS

Most of the world's plains are flat grasslands, with only a few trees to break up the landscape. Most of them stretch, like a shimmering ocean, as far as the eye can see.

In the cooler parts of the world, people have farmed the plains since early times. The rich **soil** provides most of the world's food harvests. Today the plains are often broken up by fences to mark out different fields. They are used to grow crops like wheat, oats and barley, or to provide food for raising animals, such as cows and sheep.

The grasslands of Africa are home to a variety of wildlife. Many species feast on the grasses, and are hunted by **predators.** Creatures like lions, elephants and zebras once roamed widely, but were hunted by people. People also turned many of their old territories into farmland. These wild animals are now confined to the few remaining areas of unspoiled plains.

▼ Trees on the **tropical** plains have thick bark to protect them against fires, and deep roots to tap underground water. Many have spikes to defend their leaves against grazing animals.

# WHERE IN THE WORLD?

Most plains lie towards the centre of the Earth's continents. Often they are situated on the inner side of high mountain ranges, and so are cut off from the sea winds that bring rain. The lack of rain means that there are no great forests on the Earth's plains, because most trees need a lot of water to grow.

The tropical plains lie in belts of hot land on either side of the **Equator.** They do not have seasons like summer and winter. Instead, they have dry and wet periods.

**Temperate** grasslands lie further away from the Equator, and are hot or cold depending on the seasons.

Different countries have different names for their plains. The Russians call their plains the **steppes.** In North America, the grasslands are called **prairies,** meaning meadows. The plains of South Africa are called **veld,** which is Dutch for field. In Africa and Australia, the grasslands are known as **savannahs.** The people of South America call their plains the **pampas** and the **campo.**

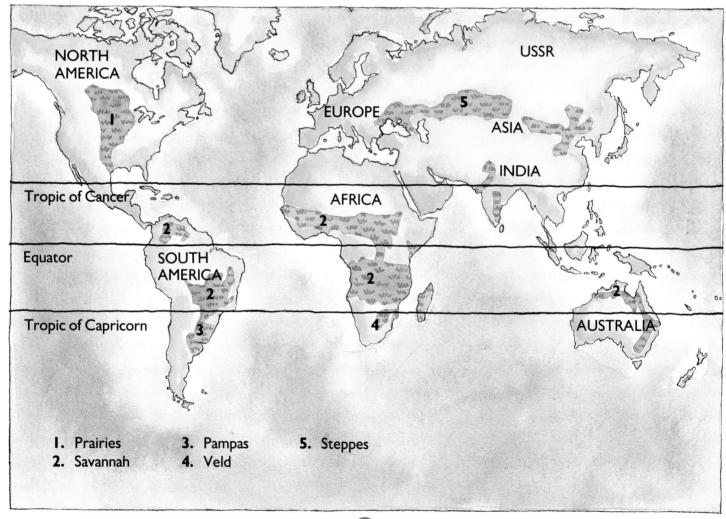

1. Prairies    3. Pampas    5. Steppes
2. Savannah    4. Veld

◀ A British combine harvester works its way through a field of ripe wheat. The blades cut, or reap, the stalks, then they shake, or thresh, the ears to release the valuable grains.

▼ In south-east Asia much of the plains are flooded to grow rice, the main food eaten by about half the people in the world. Most of the back-breaking work is still done by hand. This woman from Java is transplanting rice.

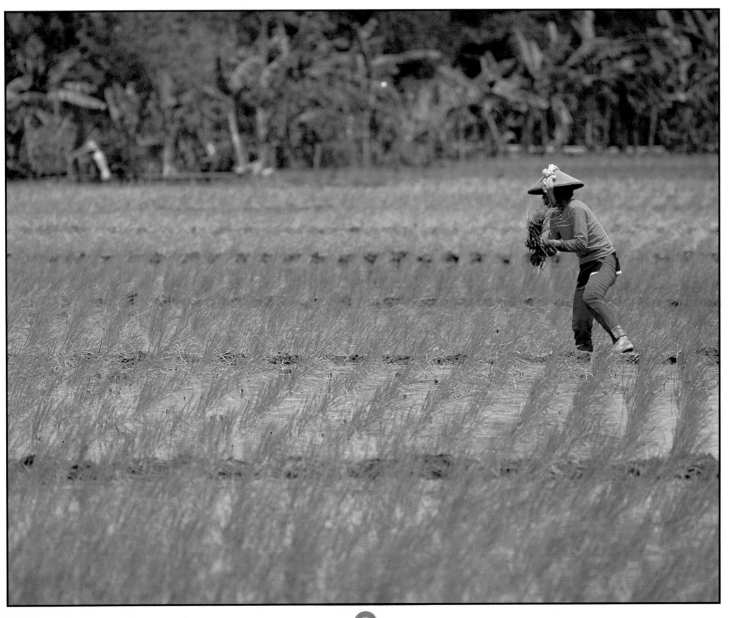

# PLANTS ON THE PLAINS

Grasses dominate the world's plains. There are about 8,000 species in all, covering about one-quarter of the Earth's surface. They grow well on the open plains because they need a great deal of light. They can survive drought, being trampled, very hot sunlight, fire and frost. If there is not enough water or heat, they just stop growing until conditions improve. Antarctica is the only area where grasses cannot thrive.

In cooler regions, the different grasses tend to remain short. In the tropical grasslands, however, they can grow to enormous heights.

Among the grasses may grow plants like dandelions, daisies and clover. Plants like lilies that grow from bulbs also thrive on the plains.

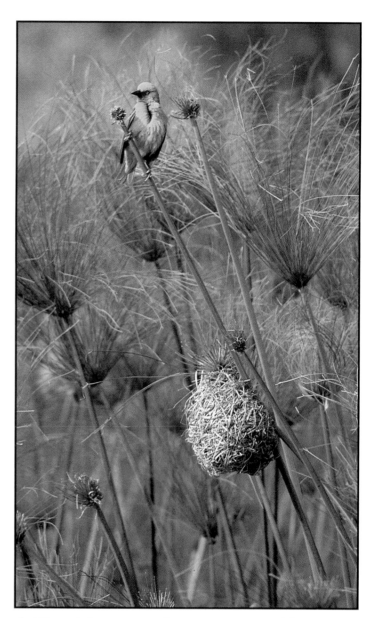

▲ The plains grasses have many uses. Here, a Cape weaver bird perches above its nest in South Africa. The male has carefully woven the bell-shaped nest from dried grasses to attract a female. The female will approve the nest, then prepare an inside lining to cushion the eggs.

◀ A swollen baobab tree rises from a sisal plantation in Madagascar. The spongy trunk stores rainwater, then shrinks in dry weather. In a drought, elephants have been known to tear off branches to reach the water hidden inside.

► A tumbleweed rolls around a dusty plain in Mexico. These plants develop rounded tops, then wither and break off at ground level in the autumn. The large, light plant then rolls around the plains, tossed about by the winds. As the weed tumbles, it scatters its seeds over a wide area. Tumbleweeds are considered a nuisance by farmers as they often pile up against fences and fill up small valleys.

# FOOD FACTS

● Grass seeds are light and easily carried by the wind. They soon colonise a patch of bare ground, sending out a network of underground stems, which sprout new leaves. Farmers soon learned to breed certain varieties to provide plentiful and cheap food crops.

● Some grasses are used to feed animals like cows and sheep. The farmer may sow a mixture of two or three kinds of grass seed, and clover. Fertiliser makes the grass grow better. In summer, the grass may be cut to make hay and silage to feed the animals in the winter.

● **Cereals** are grasses that provide food for people. Varieties include oats, maize, wheat, barley, millet and rice. Popcorn, cornflakes, and corn oil for frying are made from maize. Wheat grains are ground into flour for bread and pasta. Porridge is made from oats.

# ANIMAL LIFE

In the wild, the plains grasses feed huge herds of **grazers.** Most grazers are **herbivores.** A great variety live in Africa, including antelopes, giraffes, rhinoceroses, elephants, and zebras. Many of these animals prefer to browse on the trees and bushes. Giraffes feed on the lower branches of the acacia, so that the thorny trees end up looking like umbrellas.

Grass leaves and seeds also feed hordes of insects like jewel-coloured butterflies and grasshoppers. The soil below is tunnelled and heaped by termites, or ants. One huge African anthill even had a village built on it.

The South American pampas is home to small grazers such as the mara and cavies, wild relations of the guinea pig. Larger animals like kangaroos and wallabies feed on the savannahs of Australia.

▲ A dung beetle tests a rabbit pellet. These beetles often roll the droppings of elephants and other large animals into smaller balls, then bury them. They lay their eggs in the dung, which provides food for their larvae.

▶ On many of the world's plains, the main protection from predators is to run fast. Some animals live in herds, like these African zebra drinking at a waterhole, so that there are plenty of eyes and ears to spot danger. A lion could be lurking behind any nearby bush.

## ANIMAL ANTICS

The South American anteater has a specially shaped snout for easing ants, termites and other grubs from the soil. It has a long whip-like tongue, which it uses to catch the insects.

Prairie dogs, or marmots, live in North America. They burrow tunnels to house their big communities, or 'cities'. One city was thought to have held up to 400 million prairie dogs. They are now rare.

# BIRDS IN THE BUSH

Birds of all different shapes and sizes live on the plains. Clouds of small birds feast on the plentiful seeds and vast numbers of insects.

The African savannah is ruled by the meat-eating vultures. They circle above the plains in search of dead flesh. Marabou storks and ravens also join in the **scavenging.** Eagles and hawks also prey on the plains.

A number of flightless birds, like the South American rhea and the Australian emu, roam the grasslands. These birds are fast runners and tend to be large: the African ostrich can grow up to 2.4 m tall. The birds live in flocks and feed on seeds, plants and even small animals.

▲ Cattle egrets live in Africa near antelope, cattle, and elephants. They perch on an animal's back to eat insects, like lice or ticks, living there. Egrets warn their hosts of any danger by flying off suddenly.

◀ Two ostriches look after their young. At one month old, the babies can run as fast as an adult – up to 64 km per hour. The ostrich can live up to 70 years and is the world's largest living bird. It has good eyesight to spot its enemies and can kick an attacker to death using the sharp nails on the two toes on each foot.

▶ An African secretary bird stamps on a grasshopper. It eats insects, frogs, lizards, small tortoises and snakes. Sometimes it flies high, drops its prey, then lands and eats it.

▼ Huge flocks of small birds, like these pink cockatoos from Australia, swoop over the grassy plains. The cockatoos mainly feed on a variety of insects, fruit, nuts and grass seeds.

# HUNTERS OF THE PLAINS

The best-known plains dwellers are the big **game** animals of Africa. They feed on the grazing animals.

Lions live in groups, or prides, of up to 30 animals on a territory. They will eat mainly wildebeest, zebras and gazelles. Other hunters include cheetahs, leopards, hyenas, jackals and serval cats.

The grey wolf once prowled the Russian steppes and the prairies of North America. It is now very rare, having been hunted because of its threat to farm animals and people. In North America, the coyote has replaced it as the main predator.

The main hunter on the pampas of South America is the cunning jaguar. It will lie in ambush and stalk for long periods to catch its prey.

## SNAKE CHARMER

The mongoose is a slim animal, rather like a ferret. Some species are famous for killing snakes. The mongoose has sharp eyesight and can usually dodge a snake's fangs. It also eats insects, rats, snails, worms and lizards. Some will smash eggs to the ground to eat them.

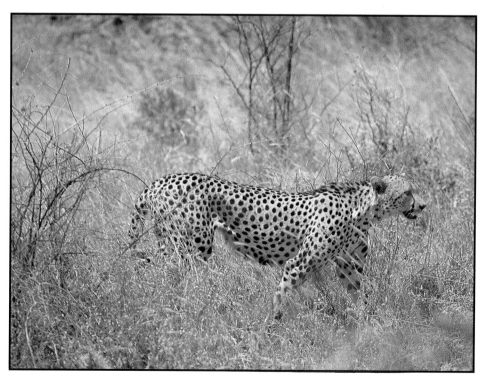

◀ The flecked coat of a cheetah **camouflages** it against the sun-dappled grasses. Cheetahs are the fastest land animals over a short distance. They can sprint at 110 km per hour, hunting mainly during the day for antelopes and gazelles.

Cheetahs are now rare as much of their old hunting grounds have been turned into farmland. Most now live in Africa. Cheetahs have also been hunted for their **pelts.** In India, the last cheetah was shot by a hunter in 1947.

► **Carrion** is left by a hunter, such as a lion, once it has eaten its fill. The scavengers then gather to share the spoils. Here, spotted hyenas and vultures pick a skeleton clean on an African plain. In the background, a solitary marabou stork waits patiently for its turn at the feast.

Scavenging birds often have featherless, bare skin on their necks and heads to help them feed more easily inside the dead animal's body.

▼ A zebra runs for its life, fleeing from a lioness. Often several lionesses will surround their prey so that it cannot escape. When it is killed, the male lions and cubs come to share the meal. Lions have few enemies, and sleep up to 20 hours a day.

# CROSSING THE PLAINS

Many of the grazing herds of the plains travel enormous distances in search of food. The wildebeest of the East African plains **migrate** every year in search of fresh feeding grounds in the river valleys. At the beginning of the dry season, the separate herds gather to start the long trek. They are often joined by groups of gazelles and zebras. The immense herds will travel up to 200 km and will often mate on the way. When the rainy season begins, they return to the open plains, where their calves will be born.

Saiga antelopes on the vast Russian steppes also ramble over very long distances, in search of fresh food and water. They are known to travel up to 350 km over the steppes in a single year.

### DID YOU KNOW?

● Sometimes a plague of locusts comes to the African plains. These insects ride on the wind in huge swarms of up to 50 million. A swarm can rapidly eat enough to feed 400 thousand people for a year.

▶ The best-known migration on the East African plains is that of the wildebeest. They travel in enormous groups of up to 1,000 animals. The lengthy journey is often very dangerous, especially when crossing a rushing river. Many animals do not survive.

▼ On the North American prairies, the bison used to migrate each year but they are now confined to **national parks.**

# PLAINS

The first peop
lived on the
years a
ate b
pe

# PEOPLES

...ple are thought to have ...e plains around 40,000 ...go. They hunted animals and ...erries and roots. Gradually, the ...ople learned to tame some animals and to harvest food crops from some of the plants. They developed ways of breeding to give new, improved plants and animals for farming from the wild varieties.

Today, food crops for humans and animals are grown in vast fields all over the world. A range of different animals are kept on the pastures for their meat, milk or skins.

In many lands, some people live on the plains as **nomads.** They usually keep herds of animals and move from place to place in search of grazing land. On the steppes of Asia, for example, the Mongols and Kazakhs keep herds of cattle, sheep and horses. The animals provide them with food, clothing and the materials to make tents.

▼ Wealthy farmers use cowboys to **ranch** cattle on the Mato Grosso plain of South America. The cowboys work on horseback and wear tough leather clothes to protect them from thorns as they ride across the plain.

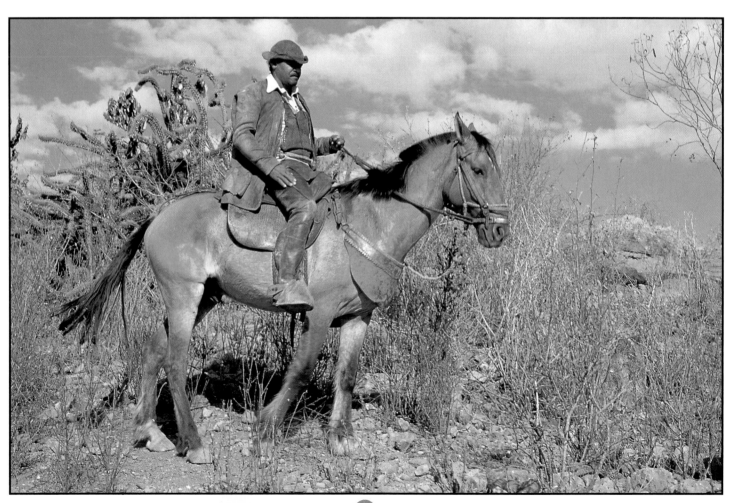

► A young Masai warrior practises a traditional dance. The Masai live on the borders of Kenya and Tanzania in East Africa. They build villages near a water supply and move on when the grass of the surrounding land has been eaten by their cattle. They mainly feed on cow's blood mixed with milk, with a few vegetables, traded from other tribes for meat and skins.

## PEOPLE FACTS

● Some of the Aboriginal people of Australia still live by hunting animals and eating wild plants. Most now live in **reserves.** In the past, Aborigines would remember long-distance routes across country by learning complex songs which mentioned important landmarks.

# PLAIN DESTRUCTION

People have greatly changed the world's plains. Long ago in the northern **hemisphere**, people cleared forests and ploughed up the grasses to make farmland. In Britain, 80 per cent of forest was felled. The wild plants and animals gave way to domestic crops and herds.

Modern farmers use chemicals, called fertilisers and pesticides, to help their crops grow better. Some of these chemicals have ruined the soil and even damaged water supplies. Overfarming also leads to **erosion**, when soil is blown or washed away.

On the tropical plains, people have also used the best land for farming. Some farmers have allowed herds to overgraze the grass and again this has caused erosion. The grass roots hold soil in place, but with grass and soil gone, only bare rock will remain and the feasting animals move on.

## DID YOU KNOW?

● Millions of bison used to roam the North American prairies. Overhunted, they now survive only in reserves.

● Small burrowing prairie dogs, which were once common, are now scarce.

● Saiga antelope once covered the Russian steppe. Few survive today.

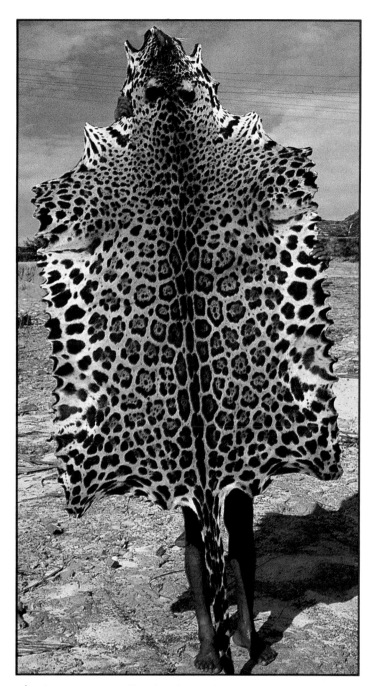

▲ A man proudly displays the hide of a jaguar. These rare animals are hunted for their high quality fur, which is made into clothes, bags and shoes. Other plains animals that have been hunted close to **extinction** to provide luxury products include the rhinoceros, the lion and the elephant. Many countries around the world now ban the import of any goods made from endangered animals.

▶ Bare soil shows through in Masai country, Kenya. Here, the herds of sheep and goats have sadly been allowed to overgraze. Where the grass has gone, soil quickly blows away. In hot countries such as Kenya, the ruined plains may soon turn into desert.

▼ Fires occur naturally on the African plains in the hot, dry season. Local trees have thick bark to protect them from the heat. The charred grasses soon grow back from the roots. Some fires harm animals and destroy crops.

# SAVE THE PLAINS

Of all the people in the world, the farmers can help most to save the plains. They can try to use chemical fertilisers more carefully so that the soil is not damaged. They can plant trees and hedges to prevent soil erosion from the wind. If any land has been overgrazed, they can fence it off to prevent animals from damaging it even further.

Farming land on plains at the edge of deserts should be **irrigated** to make best use of water supplies. Crops that are specially adapted to the dry conditions should be grown. Every few years, farmers must leave parts of their land unfarmed so that the soil can recover its richness.

The wild animals of the plains also need protection. In Africa, many elephants have been killed for their **ivory** tusks, while the spotted cats are gunned down by **poachers** for their pelts. Most African countries have put these animals into national parks and set up armed patrols to protect them. People must refuse to buy products made from ivory and animal fur to stop the trade.

▼ A family of giraffes run across an African plain. Giraffes must watch out for predators. They sleep for only about 20 minutes each night, divided into three or four short naps. Adult giraffes will eat mainly leaves and twigs, up to six metres above the ground.

▼ Large areas of Africa have been set aside for wild animals to live in peace. However, the rhinoceros is still hunted secretly by poachers. There are not very many of these animals left alive on the plains of Africa today. Rhinos browse on grass, twigs and leaves. White egrets eat the insects that live on rhinos, and those turned up in the soil as they walk along.

## PLAIN PERSUASION

### Support campaigns
There are many groups trying to stop the killing of plains wildlife. They need money and support to continue. Watch out for news on television, the radio, newspapers and magazines for how you can help.

### Stop the trade
Explain to people why you yourself would not wear fur clothes, or buy products made from rare species.

# RED LEAF AND THE GREAT BUFFALO BULL

*For thousands of years, people have told stories about the world around them. Often these stories try to explain something that people do not understand, like how the world began. This story, told by the Cheyenne Indians of North America, tries to explain how the group of stars we know as the Pleiades came to be.*

Long ago, a girl named Red Leaf lived in a teepee on the plains with her seven adopted brothers. Every day, six of the brothers would go out hunting, while the youngest, who was known as Little Brother, would stay behind to chop wood and fetch water. Red Leaf cooked the meat that the brothers brought home, and made and mended their moccasins and clothes. They all took care of each other and were very happy.

One day, six of the brothers went out hunting, and Little Brother went to fetch water, leaving Red Leaf alone in the camp. On his return, Red Leaf was gone, and there were signs of a great struggle. From the hoof-prints, Little Brother knew that the Great Buffalo Bull, who ruled over all the buffalo, had stolen Red Leaf.

When his brothers returned, Little Brother told them his story. All the brothers were afraid of the Great Buffalo Bull, but they knew they must save their precious sister.

The seven brothers built a series of four strong corrals, one inside the other, so that they would have a safe place to run to if they managed to bring back Red Leaf. Little Brother went out and collected anthills in his cloak. He sprinkled them in a steady line, all along the inside ground of the innermost corral.

Then, taking up their very special magic medicine sacks, the seven brothers bravely set off, following the dusty trail of the Great Buffalo Bull's enormous hoofprints.

They travelled for a long time. At last, they came to a hill overlooking the vast plain. Below them, covering the plain as far as they could see, stretched the buffalo herd. Right in the middle was a wide open space, where the Great Buffalo Bull stood, with poor Red Leaf lying nearby.

"We must get a message to Red Leaf, to tell her we are here," said the oldest brother. He brought out his magic medicine sack, which was made from the skin of a blackbird. As he held it in his hand, it turned into a living blackbird and flew off into the centre of the herd, right to the place where Red Leaf lay.

But before the blackbird could deliver the message, it heard the Great Buffalo Bull bellow furiously: "Get away, spy!"

The earth shook, as the Great Buffalo Bull pawed the ground, and the blackbird flew off in fear.

The second brother took out his coyote skin medicine sack. As he held it, it turned into a living coyote, which set off boldly through the buffalo herd until it managed to reach the very place where little Red Leaf lay.

"Get away, spy!" roared the Great Buffalo Bull in a terrible fury, and the cowardly coyote swiftly turned tail and slunk away.

The third brother's medicine sack was made from the skin of a little yellow bird. The bird was so tiny that it reached Red Leaf without the Great Buffalo Bull noticing.

"Red Leaf," whispered the bird, in its tiny voice. "Pull your cloak over your head and wait for your seven brothers to rescue you."

When the little yellow bird returned, Little Brother took out his gopher skin medicine sack. As he placed the skin on the ground, it turned into a living gopher and began to dig right under the herd. Little Brother followed the gopher along its tunnel and came up under Red Leaf's cloak. He led her down the tunnel, leaving her cloak over the hole. Then Red Leaf and her brothers ran as fast as they could to the corrals.

It was not long before the Great Buffalo Bull noticed something was amiss. He pushed Red Leaf's cloak aside with his hoof and discovered the secret tunnel below. Bellowing furiously, he charged off at once in the direction of the brothers' camp, with the rest of the herd hard on his heels. In no time at all, the Great Buffalo Bull was standing outside the corral with his whole herd gathered around him.

"Give me back my Red Leaf!" roared the Great Buffalo Bull.

Inside the corral, the brothers and their sister trembled with fear.

The Great Buffalo Bull began to charge the first corral. Soon, the logs lay scattered at his feet.

"Give me back my Red Leaf," he bellowed again.

"Let me go to him and the rest of you will be spared," brave Red Leaf begged her brothers.

But Little Brother insisted that they would all be safe and sound.

It was not long before the Great Buffalo Bull had tossed aside the logs of the next three corrals. But, when he came to the line of anthills, he found that every grain of sand had turned into a huge rock. The whole herd charged at these from every side, until it seemed that they would surely reach Red Leaf and the seven brothers, who quaked inside.

"Have no fear," said Little Brother, as he shot an arrow into the sky. A tree appeared, reaching skywards.

Little Brother helped his sister climb into the branches and the other six brothers followed.

As Little Brother swung himself last into the tree, the Great Buffalo Bull breached the anthills. He charged at the tree, taking huge chunks out of its trunk. Each piece the Bull tore off immediately joined back, and the tree remained as good as new.

As for Red Leaf and her seven brothers, they kept climbing the tree until they reached the sky. And you can still see them there. Red Leaf is the main star, and Little Brother is the smallest one, over to one side.

# TRUE OR FALSE?

Which of these facts are true and which ones are false?
If you have read this book carefully, you will know the answers.

1. Tropical lands have spring, summer, autumn and winter.

2. A small mongoose can catch and kill a snake.

3. Popcorn, cornflakes, and corn oil for frying are made from barley.

4. Prairie dogs live in a network of tunnels called a city.

5. South American cowboys wear clothes made from woven grasses.

6. There are about one million species of grass in the world.

7. Giraffes will sleep for up to 14 hours every day.

8. The ostrich can live up to 70 years.

9. A swarm of locusts can rapidly devour enough food to feed 400 thousand people for one year.

10. Scavenging birds like vultures often have bare skin on their heads.

ANSWERS: 1. False 2. True 3. False 4. True 5. False 6. False 7. False 8. False 9. True 10. True

# GLOSSARY

**Campo** is a tropical grassland in South America.

**Camouflage** hides an animal against its surroundings to protect it from predators, and can help it to capture prey.

**Carrion** is dead flesh.

**Cereals** are members of the grass family, which have been developed by people to provide food.

**Equator** is the imaginary line round the Earth, halfway between the North and the South Pole.

**Erosion** is the wearing away of soil or rock by wind, rain and floods, ice or frost.

**Extinction** occurs when the last one of an animal or plant species dies out. This often happens when animals are overhunted by people or other species, or when they lose their food, or a feeding place.

**Game** animals are wild animals which are hunted by humans.

**Grazers** are animals that feed on grasses or other plants.

**Hemisphere** is one half of the Earth. There are two halves: the northern and the southern hemispheres.

**Herbivores** eat only grass and other plants. They have special teeth with ridged surfaces to grind the grass into small pieces.

**Irrigate** is artificially to water land that naturally tends to be dry. Water is often channelled through ditches.

**Ivory** is what makes up elephants' tusks, as well as those of some other animals. It was once used to make piano keys.

**Migrate** means to move from one area to another. This often takes place once a year as the seasons change and animals and birds look for fresh supplies of food and a spell in a warmer climate.

● **National parks** are large areas of land protected by law, where the landscape cannot be changed and the birds and animals cannot be harmed by hunters or collectors.

● **Nomads** are people who travel following animal herds, which provide food and materials for clothes and tent-making.

● **Pampas** are the temperate grasslands of South America. Pampa is the Spanish word for a plain.

● **Pelt** is the skin or fur of an animal.

● **Poachers** are people who kill animals illegally to make money from selling their meat, skins, horns, tusks or other parts.

● **Prairies** are the temperate grasslands of North America.

● **Predators** are any animals that hunt and kill other animals.

● **Ranch** is to breed and raise cattle.

● **Reserve** is a special area set aside under the laws of a country for certain people or animals to live in.

● **Savannah** is the name given to tropical grasslands in both Africa and Australia.

● **Scavenging** is when animals or birds feed on the remains of dead animals that they have not hunted for themselves.

● **Soil** is the top layer of ground in which plants grow. It is made up of ground-down particles of rock.

● **Steppes** are the temperate grasslands of both south-east Europe and Asia.

● **Temperate** describes the mild climate that is found in bands of land on either side of the tropical area.

● **Tropical** describes the hot climate around the Equator.

● **Veld** is the temperate grassland of South Africa.

# INDEX